Usborne
Art Activity Book

Sam Baer & Rosie Hore

Designed by
Mary Cartwright & Alice Reese

Illustrated by
Fred Blunt, Adam Larkum, Marianne Oldʌ...
Carles Ballesteros, Ilaria Fa
& 28 famous a

Edited by
Rosie Dickins

In association with
The National Gallery, London

CONTENTS

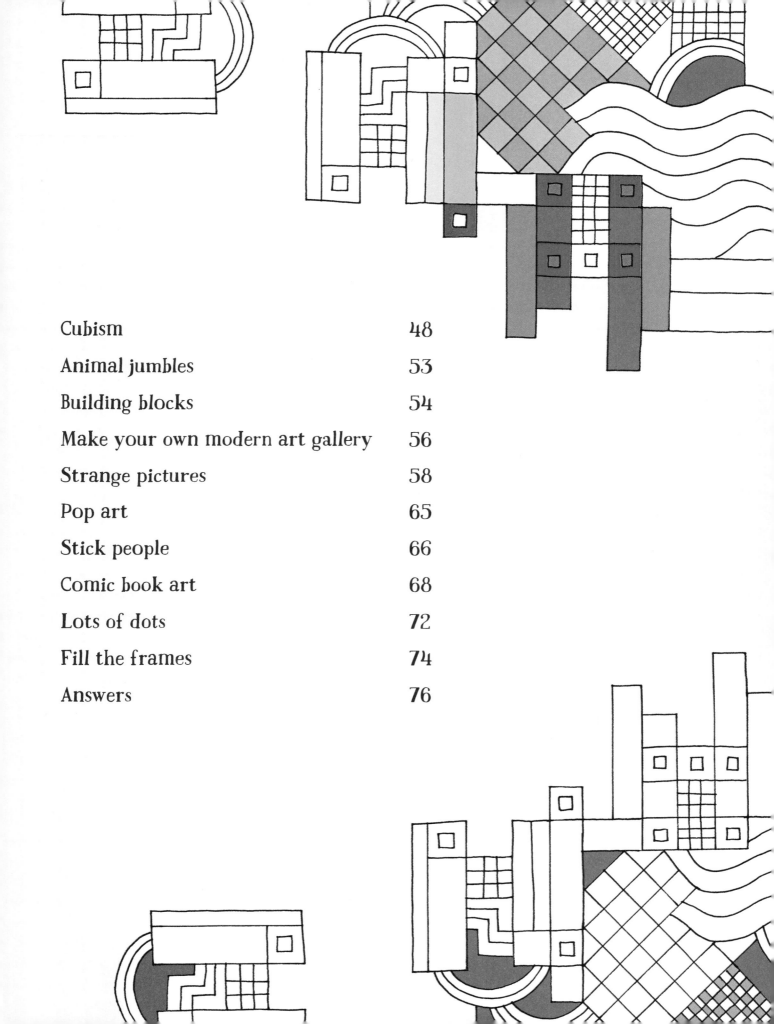

ARTIST'S STUDIO

Five hundred years ago, if you wanted to become an artist, you had to start as a trainee or 'apprentice' in the studio of a *master* artist. Some apprentices left home to join a studio before they were even 10 years old.

Starting off

New apprentices began by doing odd jobs, such as cleaning brushes and mixing paint. They had to learn the names of the exotic ingredients which made up the different colours.

How many of the ingredients below can you find in this wordsearch?

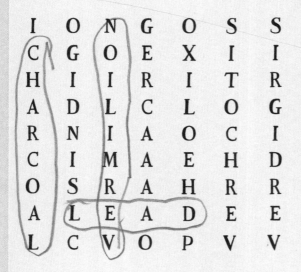

```
I  O  N  G  O  S  S
C  G  O  E  X  I  I
H  I  I  R  I  T  R
A  D  L  C  L  O  G
R  N  I  A  O  C  I
C  I  M  A  E  H  D
O  S  R  A  H  R  R
A  L  E  A  D  E  E
L  C  V  O  P  V  V
```

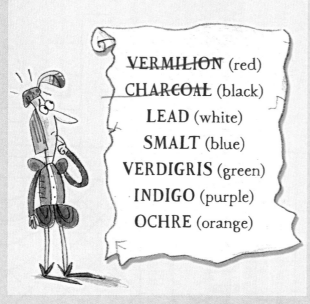

VERMILION (red)
CHARCOAL (black)
LEAD (white)
SMALT (blue)
VERDIGRIS (green)
INDIGO (purple)
OCHRE (orange)

Pouncing

Apprentices often used a method called pouncing to transfer drawings.

First, they pricked tiny holes in the original drawing. Then, they laid it over the new picture and dusted charcoal over the top, leaving marks underneath the holes.

Finish this copy of the portrait using the charcoal marks.

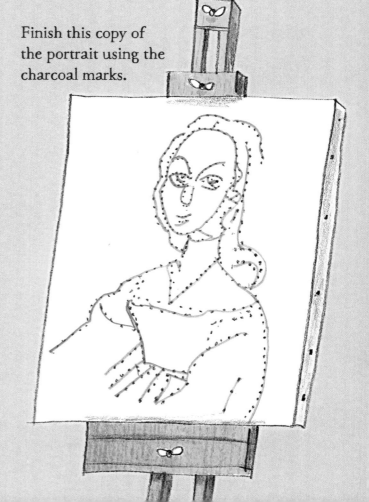

Filling in

Some master artists would paint only the main figures in a picture, leaving the rest to be filled in by the studio's apprentices. Add your own background to this picture to finish it off.

Did you know?

Sometimes, master artists didn't work on a painting at all. But their apprentices were so good, nobody could tell the difference.

Top models

Apprentices practised by drawing each other. Which of these apprentices has copied the model's pose most accurately?

Leo

Marco

Giovanni

PORTRAITS

Portraits are works of art – painted or sculpted – that aim to show how someone looks, or what their personality is like.

A The lady in this picture is also the artist who painted it. This type of portrait is known as a 'self portrait'.

B This portrait of a man wearing a gold wreath comes from the case of an ancient Egyptian mummy. It shows what the man inside looked like.

E This lady lived over 100 years ago. She was painted in a style, known as 'Impressionism', which was fashionable at the time.

C This young boy was named after his dad, whose portrait you can also see on this page.

D This painting shows a former ruler, known for being loyal or 'steadfast'.

Missing titles

Can you guess which portrait goes with each of the paintings listed below?

D Johann the Steadfast (1509)
by Lucas Cranach the Elder

A Self Portrait (after 1782)
by Elisabeth Vigée Le Brun

B A Man with a Wreath
(artist unknown)

C Johann Friedrich the Magnanimous (1509)
by Lucas Cranach the Elder

E Portrait of Elena Carafa (c.1875)
by Edgar Degas

Dressed to impress

The self portrait on the opposite page shows a lady with various props and accessories. Can you rearrange the letters below to spell out some of them?

ALPTTEE   SWATR ATH   SLOWFER

SHRBUES   WHSLA   SGNIRERA

Did you know?

One of the oldest portraits in the world is a carving of a woman's face, made in central Europe around 26,000 years ago.

Artistic licence

This boy is having his portrait painted, but the artist has decided to change a few details.

Can you spot all five differences?

Faces to finish

Most portraits focus on the features that make someone unique. Make your own unique portraits by drawing different hairstyles, accessories and expressions onto the faces below.

Imagine a background for this old family portrait.
Draw it in, then colour the whole picture.

You could give this
portrait a stylish outfit.

Give these
portraits faces
and hair.

Give fantastic hairstyles
to these bald heads.

MAKE YOUR OWN PORTRAIT GALLERY

Try filling this frame with a picture of yourself or a character from your imagination.

What expression will you give to this royal portrait?

Fill this frame with a superhero or an alien.

Instead of drawing a face, you could cut out and stick in a photograph from an old magazine or newspaper – then doodle over the top.

STILL LIFES

Paintings of food, plants and other still objects are known as 'still lifes'. This imaginary still life shows flowers from different seasons, all in bloom at the same time.

Flowers in a Vase (1792)
by Paulus Theodorus van Brussel

Can you spot two flitting butterflies?

Odd one out

Which of these details *doesn't* belong in the painting?

Did you know?

Tulips were first introduced to Europe around 500 years ago – leading to a craze known as 'tulipmania'. Tulip bulbs were so rare and so in demand that, for a while, they were more expensive than buying a house.

Expensive

Not as expensive

Match the meaning

Some still lifes are like coded messages, full of objects with symbolic meanings.

Can you match all the objects on the right to the numbers of meanings in the list?

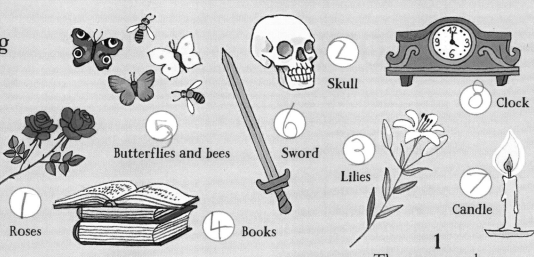

Butterflies and bees

Skull (2)

Clock (8)

Sword (6)

Lilies (3)

Candle (7)

Roses

(1)

Books (4)

(5)

1
These suggest love and romance.

2
This is a sign of death.

3
These suggest hope and fragility.

4
These show wisdom and knowledge.

5
These are meant to be a sign of purity.

6
This means power and protection.

7
When lit, this object is a sign of hope.

8
This shows the passing of time.

Flowers to colour

Finish off this still life by adding more flowers, some fluttering butterflies and eggs in the nest. Then colour it in.

COLOURS

Some artists deliberately use certain colours to make you feel different moods or feelings.

Vincent van Gogh painted this picture of sunflowers for his friend, Paul Gauguin. He used lots of yellow, which for him was the colour of joy and happiness.

Sunflowers (1888)
by Vincent van Gogh

Combing the hair (1896)
by Edgar Degas

By using lots of red, Edgar Degas made this indoor scene feel hot and uncomfortable.

Did you know?

For thousands of years, artists used a paint known as 'mummy brown' – made from ancient Egyptian mummies.

Moody tones

Choose a colour for each of these scenes. Then colour them in with different tones of that colour, to conjure up a different atmosphere.

Red can be warmth, anger or passion.

Yellow can mean joy or happiness.

Orange is warm and energetic.

Pink can show love or caring.

Blue can be cold, calm, or sad.

Green is for envy or jealousy.

Paint hunt

Lead the apprentice through the maze, collecting paints for his impatient master. Make sure you collect one of each colour.

Avoid any bottles of Emerald green, it's poisonous!

● Cobalt violet   ● Prussian blue   ● Vermilion red   ● Chrome yellow

Orange (1923)
by Wassily Kandinsky

Russian artist Wassily Kandinsky believed shapes and colours could express feelings. In this painting, he combined different shapes and colours to create a feeling of excitement, energy and movement.

Kandinsky believed...

 ...blues and circles were calm and still.

...yellows and triangles were even more energetic.

...reds and squares were energetic.

...sloped lines suggested movement, while straight lines suggested stillness.

Did you know?

Some experts think Kandinsky had a rare condition that let him 'see' sound and 'hear' colour.

You could make a Kandinsky-style picture at the back of the book, using the shapes from the sticker pages.

Warm and cold

Red, yellow and orange are the colours of fire, sunshine and warm things, while blue, green and white are the colours of water, ice and cool things. When you see them side-by-side, warm and cool colours create vibrant contrasts. Try finishing the picture below by putting warm and cool colours together.

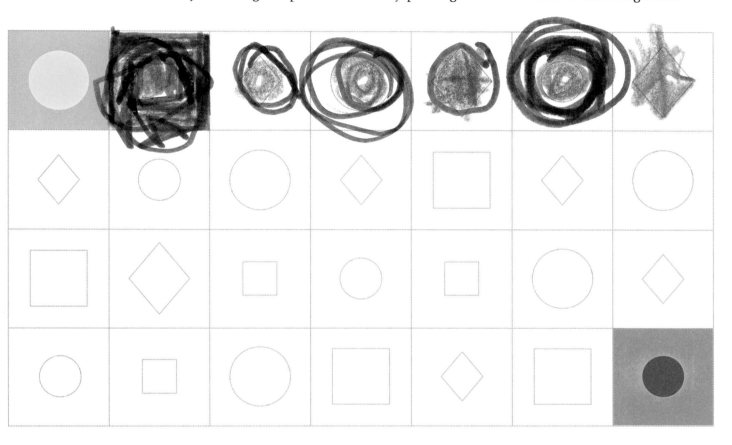

Colour illusions

Colours can also trick the eye. See for yourself below. Look at the black dot in the middle of the coloured rectangle and count to 30, slowly. Then look at the dot in the white rectangle and count again. Can you see a ghostly version or 'after-image' of the coloured rectangle?

 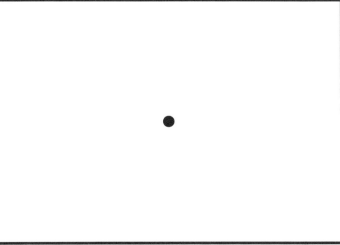

FIT FOR A KING

This 600-year-old painting shows a former king of England, kneeling before Mary and Jesus and a host of angels. Notice the huge amounts of blue. At the time, it was one of the most expensive colours – even more costly than gold – showing the painting must have been made for someone very wealthy.

Spiritual colours

To people at the time, certain colours also had spiritual meanings.

Can you spot...

A green cloak

Green shows growth, new life and hope.

A gold blanket

Gold suggests holiness and heavenly light.

White robes

White is meant to show purity.

The Wilton Diptych (1395-9)
by an unknown artist

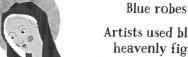

Blue robes

Artists used blue for heavenly figures, because it's the colour of the sky. This blue was made from a rare gem called lapis lazuli, which came all the way from Afghanistan.

16

Colour in these angels using blue for their robes.

LANDSCAPES

Artists use different techniques to create the atmosphere of a particular place. Dutch artist Vincent van Gogh painted this wheat field in the south of France. His bold brushstrokes make the wheat look as if it's swaying in the wind, beneath a swirling sky.

This picture below shows a field and trees too, but it looks very different. The artist John Constable was painting a scene near his home in the English countryside.

A Wheatfield, with Cypresses (1889)
by Vincent van Gogh

The Cornfield (1826)
by John Constable

Shifting horizons

The line where the land meets the sky in a landscape is called the horizon. By placing the horizon in different places, artists can shift your focus towards the earth or the sky.

In Constable's picture, the horizon looks as if it's very far away. The picture below, by Richard Parkes Bonington, has a low horizon with lots of sky.

La Ferté (c.1825)
by Richard Parkes Bonington

Pictures of the sea or beach are also called seascapes. In seascapes, the horizon is usually where the sea meets the sky, rather than the land.

Water lilies

Monet painted this landscape of the lily pond in his garden with a rough style, making it look like an on-the-spot sketch.

Colour your own lily pond by filling the rest of this page with rough, scribbly shapes. You could add drooping branches and leaves in the background, and colourful lilies floating on the water.

Did you know?

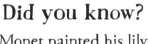

Monet painted his lily pond over 250 times.

Finish this landscape and give it a title.

Give this landscape some colours. They don't have to be realistic.

You could add trees, flowers or houses to this scene.

In these tiny frames, you could focus on one detail. Try drawing the tip of a mountain, a branch of a tree, or even just a few leaves.

MAKE YOUR OWN LANDSCAPE GALLERY

Fill this frame with an imaginary landscape,
starting with the horizon line. You could colour
the sky using swirls and curls, like Van Gogh.

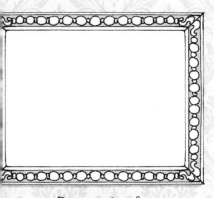

Draw a view from a
window here.

Add more ships and waves
to this seascape.

Doodle a desert island
in this frame.

PERSPECTIVE

Perspective is a set of rules artists use for giving flat, 2D pictures the illusion of depth – or 3 dimensions.

The Avenue at Middelharnis follows strict guidelines to create a dramatic perspective. You can see how it was done in the diagram below.

The Avenue at Middelharnis
(1689)
by Meindert Hobbema

Lines that slope towards the horizon, called orthogonals, create the effect of things receding into the distance.

The orthogonals meet at the 'vanishing point' – that's the point where things become too tiny to see.

Vanishing point

Horizon

In the distance

Now it's your turn. Draw some more trees following the same guidelines. You could add tiny buildings to the horizon and some people on the road...

The Annunciation, with Saint Emidius (1486)
by Carlo Crivelli

Using perspective helps artists to paint buildings accurately. Here, the bricks were painted along orthogonals. Can you follow them back to a red hat in the background? That's the vanishing point.

Up close

Can you spot all these details?

A carpet on a wall

A hanging bird cage

A model of a town

A woman in blue

A child in a white cap

An apple and a vegetable called a gourd

A dovecote

Impossible perspective

Everything in this picture looks a bit strange. Can you identify six mistakes in perspective, to show why the artist has got it wrong?

GODS AND MONSTERS

This scene comes from an ancient Greek myth about a god called Bacchus. One day, while he was out in his chariot, he spotted a princess watching a boat sail away. It was Ariadne, who had been abandoned by a heartless prince. Bacchus fell in love with her on sight. Eventually they married, and he tossed Ariadne's crown into the sky, where it became a ring of stars.

Bacchus and Ariadne (1520-23) by Titian

Titian's painting combines different parts of the story. Can you spot:

a chariot pulled by cheetahs

a ring of stars

Bacchus, leaping from his chariot, wearing a crown of vine leaves

Princess Ariadne, dressed in red, white and blue robes

a boat sailing away in the distance

Guess the goddess

The ancient Greeks believed in lots of gods and goddesses. Can you match each goddess on the right to her description below?

Aphrodite – goddess of love and beauty

Athena – goddess of war and wisdom

Artemis – goddess of wild animals and hunting

Mythical monsters

Many Greek myths describe strange creatures, some of them part human and part animal. Finish drawing the mythical creatures below.

In Titian's picture, you can see a 'satyr' – a boy with the legs of a goat.

I'm Pegasus, a flying horse. Draw me some wings.

I'm Medusa – part-woman, part-snake. Give me snakes for hair.

I'm a centaur – half-man, half-horse. Doodle me a mane and tail, then colour me in.

I'm a harpy – part-woman, part-bird. I need sharp claws.

I'm a siren. I'm often shown with a fish tail, like a mermaid.

Did you know?

Titian's picture was painted for the Duke of Ferrara in Italy. The cheetahs were probably based on ones in the Duke's private zoo.

Create-a-creature

You could draw your own mythical monsters in the empty frames on pages 74-75. They could have wings, horns, or anything else you can imagine...

KNIGHTS & DRAGONS

This 600-year-old painting shows a scene from the story of Saint George. The story goes that Saint George was sent to rescue a princess from a deadly dragon. George fought the dragon and managed to wound it with his lance. Then, the princess captured the dragon by tying her belt around its neck.

Saint George and the Dragon (c.1470)
by Paolo Uccello

Did you know?

Saint George is thought to have been a Roman soldier, who lived over 1,700 years ago.

Out of order

Below are some more scenes from the story. Put them in the correct order by numbering the circles.

26

The path to victory

Can you guide Saint George safely through the maze to reach the dragon and save the princess?

Avoid rocky mountains, dark forests and hungry giants.

To battle!

Saint George and the dragon have started to fight. What are they saying to one another? Complete the scene by adding your own words and doodles.

Give the dragon more fiery breath.

You could protect Saint George by giving him a shield.

Give the saint a sword. He'll need one!

Draw smoke puffing out from the dragon's nostrils.

I'll never surrender!

die mr. dragon!

AT THE RACES

George Stubbs is best known for his paintings of horses. The most famous is this painting of a racehorse called Whistlejacket. It focuses on the horse and its bold pose – without any distracting background details.

Whistlejacket (c.1762) by George Stubbs

Stubbs painted Whistlejacket almost lifesize. Here's someone looking at it, to scale.

The famous racehorse

Whistlejacket was a prize-winning racehorse who lived 250 years ago. He was named after a popular cold remedy at the time.

Tacking up

Complete these pictures of racehorses and their riders so they match each other.

The race begins

WHISTLEJACKET

GIMCRACK

MOLLY LONGLEGS

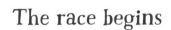

It's time to race... Whistlejacket runs along 1 section in the time that Gimcrack runs along 2 sections, and Molly Longlegs runs along 3 sections. Who will win?

MOLLY

wins the race!

Did you know?

Stubbs was fascinated by 'anatomy' – the study of how bodies are made. He drew horses' skeletons to learn more about their bodies.

Horse anatomy

How many parts of a horse's body can you circle in this winner's rosette?

29

ON THE ICE

This winter scene by Dutch artist Hendrick Avercamp was made during the 'Little Ice Age' – a time when winters were much colder, and rivers often froze over.

It shows all kinds of people gathered to skate on the ice. There are lots of little details to spot – from children playing to skaters toppling over.

This castle didn't exist – Avercamp painted it from his imagination.

A Winter Scene with Skaters near a Castle (c.1608-9)
by Hendrick Avercamp

A man putting on skates

People slipping on the ice

Lots to spot

Can you find these details in the picture?

A child in a white cap

Couples skating hand in hand

A horse and sleigh

Frost fair

When rivers froze, people would hold 'frost fairs' on the ice, with games, sleigh rides, puppet shows and food stalls.

Did you know?

Avercamp never learned to speak – probably because he was deaf.

Kit us out with hats, scarves and skates.

Word challenge

How many words can you make using only letters from the word: 'WINTERTIME'?

Will you decorate my sleigh and add a passenger?

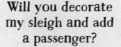

Sweets and treats

What's on the menu? Fill in the blanks to find out.

Snowmen

Spot six differences between these two snowmen.

Menu
G_NG_RBR__D
SP_C_D _PPL_S
PL_M C_K_S
H_T P__S
FR__T _ND N_TS

Clue: the missing letters are all vowels (A, E, I, O or U).

FABULOUS FASHION

In the past, people often showed off their wealth and style by posing for portraits in their best outfits. It took the artist twelve years to paint this portrait of Madame Moitessier, the wife of a wealthy banker. But he made sure she kept her outfit up to date, so that his picture would show the latest fashions.

Madame Moitessier (1856)
by Jean-Auguste-Dominique Ingres

The painting is full of luxurious accessories. Can you find:

2 fans

2 gold bracelets with red gemstones

1 ring

1 brooch

1 gold necklace

Timeless fashion

These models are wearing stylish outfits from different times and places. Can you match each one to the right description, writing A, B or C in the circles?

A. Egyptian

B. Victorian

C. Medieval

2 ◯   3 ◯

1 ◯

Fashion designer

How would you style Madame Moitessier?
Decorate these outfits, then colour them in.

You could give
each dress
a flowery
pattern...

...or add bows
and frills.

Add jewellery
and ribbons to
her hair.

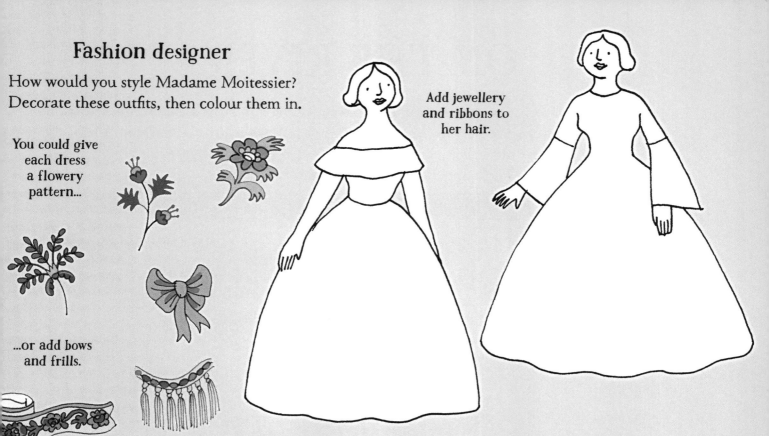

Out of place

The picture below is a copy of a
portrait of Madame Moitessier from
1851 – but with five things added that
don't belong. Can you spot them?

Mirror, mirror

Notice how Madame Moitessier and her
reflection don't quite match. The artist painted
her reflection at a different angle so he could
show her face from the side too.

Can you match
this lady to the
right reflection
below?

A   B   C

33

ON THE RIVER

French artist Pierre-Auguste Renoir used bold colour combinations to make this river boat catch your eye. See how the boat seems to pop out against the blue water. When certain colours are put side by side, they make each other look brighter and bolder. These are known as 'complementary colours'.

The Skiff (1875)
by Pierre-Auguste Renoir

Complementary colouring

There are three main pairs of complementary colours...

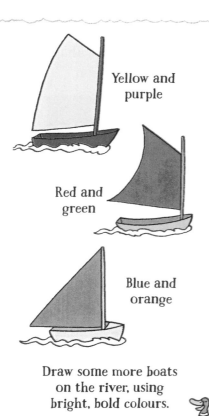

Yellow and purple

Red and green

Blue and orange

Draw some more boats on the river, using bright, bold colours.

A skiff is a small river boat.

Colour this sail with complementary colours.

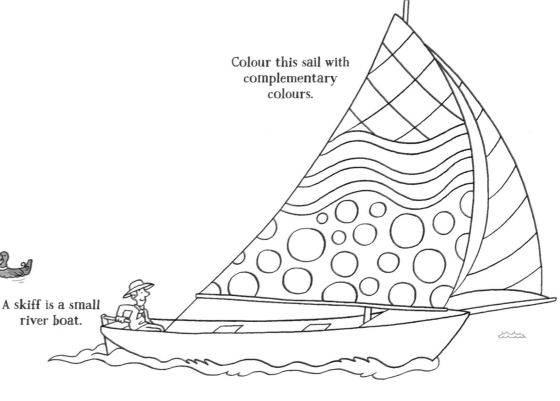

Bare boats

Can you help kit out these boats?

Which sail would be the most eye-catching?

Which oar would look the brightest?

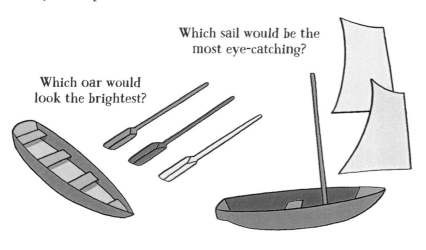

Shadow ships

Draw a line from each ship to its matching shadow.

You could fill the sails with colourful patterns.

Sail search

Find the words hidden in the sail.

SKIFF   LAKE   OAR
BOAT   ROW   SAIL

The words can be read left to right, right to left, top to bottom, or diagonally.

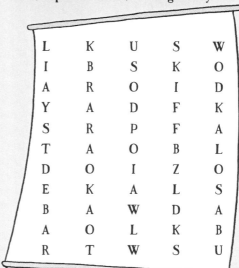

L	K	U	S	W
I	B	S	K	O
A	R	O	I	D
Y	A	D	F	K
S	R	P	F	A
T	A	O	B	L
D	O	D	Z	O
E	K	I	L	S
B	A	W	D	A
A	O	L	K	B
R	T	W	S	U

Did you know?

Renoir often painted on the banks of the River Seine in France. At one point, some people thought he was spying on them and he was nearly thrown in.

MAKE YOUR OWN STICKER ART GALLERY

You can make your own art exhibition here, using stickers from the sticker pages.

Some of the masterpieces in this gallery are hundreds of years old.

I wonder if I'll ever become a famous artist.

SUMMERTIME

French artist Georges Seurat painted this famous scene of workers relaxing on the banks of the River Seine in Paris. He used little dabs of colour to give the air and water a hazy shimmer, suggesting the intense heat of summer in the city.

In profile

Most of the people in the painting are shown in profile, which means we only see their faces from the side. Which one of these profiles matches the face on the left?

A

B

C

Bathers at Asnières (1884)
by Georges Seurat

Did you know?

This painting is huge: 3 metres (nearly 10 feet) wide. When it was first exhibited, people were shocked. Big paintings were meant to show grand historical subjects, not everyday life.

On the river bank

This man is getting dressed again after a cool dip – can you work out which pile of clothes belongs to him?

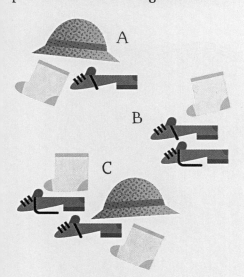

A

B

C

Spotting challenge

Take a closer look at the painting...

How many boats are on the river?

Can you find the little brown dog?

Can you spot billowing smoke from a factory chimney?

How many orange hats can you spot?

In the water

Seurat used contrasting dots to make some of the colours look more vibrant. If you look closely, there are tiny dabs of blue on the boy in the water's orange hat. Try it yourself here – you could start with the sunhats.

DREAM WORLDS

Around 100 years ago, some artists tried to paint what was in their imaginations, rather than what they saw in everyday life. This became known as Symbolism.

Ophelia among the Flowers (c.1905-8)
by Odilon Redon

French Symbolist Odilon Redon filled this picture with soft, smudgy shapes, making it feel dreamy and unreal. It shows Ophelia – a character from William Shakespeare's play *Hamlet* – and a stream which she's strewn with flowers.

Theatrical flowers

In *Hamlet*, the flowers Ophelia picks all have hidden meanings. Can you unscramble the names to discover which flower has which meaning?

NPAYS
Thoughtfulness

ISAYD
Innocence

LIVEOT
Faithfulness

ORMSERAY
Remembering

LENNFE
Flattery

Cloud shapes

Redon said he was inspired by the shapes
of clouds, because he saw 'strange beings,
fantastic and marvellous visions' in them.
What can you imagine in these cloud shapes?
Doodle whatever you can think of.

Magical monsters

Sometimes, Redon dreamed up strange monsters:
one-eyed cyclops, demons and spiders with human
faces. Try finishing these monsters yourself. You
could start by adding eyes, horns or wings.

IN THE JUNGLE

This painting by Henri Rousseau shows a fantasy jungle scene. But Rousseau never visited a real jungle – in fact, he never even left France. The tiger may have been inspired by a trip to the zoo, or from seeing a picture made by another artist.

Surprised! (1891)
by Henri Rousseau

Spot the plants

Many of the plants that make up Rousseau's jungle were based on house plants. Can you spot each of these plants in his painting?

Jungle jumble

Each of the words below was made by mixing the names of two animals together. What are the names of the original animals?

CROCOPOTAMUS

ORANGUNKEY

PARROPARD

ELEPHOCEROS

PYTHORILLA

Rousseau's tiger has lost his stripes. Draw something to take their place.
Then, add jungle vines, leaves, flowers and trees for the tiger to hide in.

DECORATIVE ART

Everyday objects that are designed to be beautiful are known as 'decorative art'. They come in lots of different shapes and styles and often feature bold patterns.

Motifs

Some artists make objects with patterns of repeated images, known as 'motifs'. Motifs can be anything from flowers to animals to geometric shapes. Continue the repeated pattern to the left by filling in the empty tiles. Then, colour them in.

Lavish accessories

Many decorative objects are inspired by nature. Match these accessories to the animals that inspired them.

These accessories are in a curvy, flowing style known as Art Nouveau, which was fashionable over one hundred years ago.

Bold shapes

Objects inspired by ancient Egyptian art, featuring straight lines and blocky shapes were popular in the 1930s, in a style known as Art Deco. Can you spot three Art Deco objects below?

Straight lines

This pattern was made in the Art Deco style.
Fill it in, using bright, bold colours.

Try finishing these Art Nouveau and Art Deco patterns. Then, colour them in.

Graphic patterns

Nearly one hundred years ago, some artists created decorative patterns using coloured lines and geometric shapes. This became known as the Bauhaus movement. Finish the Bauhaus carpet below by doodling in more lines and geometric shapes.

CUBISM

The still life below is meant to show a tabletop from several viewpoints at the same time. This style of art, known as Cubism, began around one hundred years ago. The artist made it by cutting shapes from different types of paper, then sticking them down to make a 'collage'.

The Bottle of Banyuls (1914)
by Juan Gris

Things to spot

Can you make out...

a bottle...

a newspaper...

a glass...

a tabletop...

...and a pipe?

Wonky portraits

Some Cubist artists painted people from multiple viewpoints, making wonky Cubist portraits. Can you work out which two viewpoints were used to make the portrait on the left?

A

B

C

D

Cubist portrait

Finish this face with stickers from the sticker pages at the back to make your own Cubist portrait.

Word jumble

Many Cubist pictures feature newspaper cuttings, tickets and labels with broken-up words on them. How many words can you make from the letters in this still life?

Cubist city

In this Cubist cityscape, the buildings are jumbled up together. Can you lead the artist through the streets to find his way home from the art gallery?

You can make a Cubist still life on the opposite page by cutting out and sticking down these pictures, patterns and textures.

ANIMAL JUMBLES

German artist Franz Marc painted *The Fox* around one hundred years ago.
It shows a pair of foxes, broken up and jumbled up, with the greenery around them.
Marc often painted animals this way to show how they were part of nature.

The Fox (1913)
by Franz Marc

Lots of foxes

Marc's jumbled-up style sometimes makes it difficult to spot how many animals there are in his paintings. Can you work out how many foxes there are below?

Expressive colours

For Marc, colours had specific meanings. Colour in this dog, using all of the colours described below.

Marc believed blue was a pure, spiritual colour...

yellow was the colour of joy and gentleness...

...and red was heavy and solid – the colour of earthly things.

BUILDING BLOCKS

The bold blocks of colour in this painting show a castle in the heat of a red and yellow sun. The artist Paul Klee often used simple shapes and colours like these to suggest the mood of a place, instead of showing it in a lifelike way.

Spot the blocks

Can you spot these blocks in the picture?

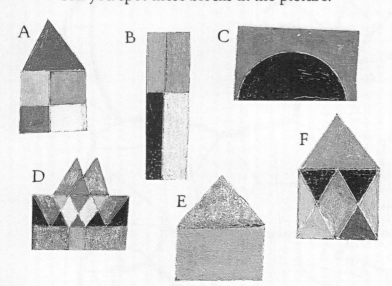

Castle and Sun (1928)
by Paul Klee

Did you know?

Klee could draw with his left and right hands. Sometimes, he used both at the same time.

54

Building a city

Fill the grid with colourful sticker shapes from the sticker pages at the back of the book to create your own blocky city.

You could try adding...

...triangles for roofs...

...small squares for windows...

...an arch across two boxes to make a bridge...

...and a sun or moon in the sky.

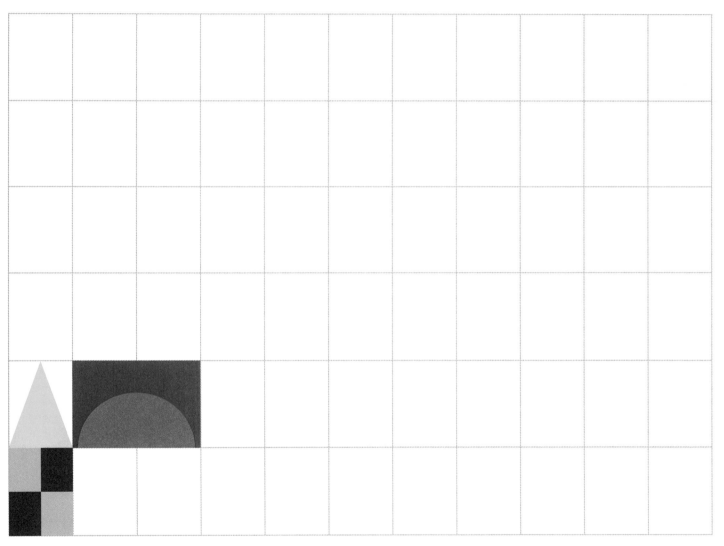

You can use colours to make your shapes stand out brightly or blend into their surroundings.

Colours that are similar, such as red and orange, blend together. Artists call these harmonising colours.

Colours that stand out from each other, such as yellow and blue, are called contrasting colours.

MAKE YOUR OWN
MODERN ART GALLERY

Fill these empty frames with your own pictures.
You could draw colourful shapes, patterns or scenes,
or you could use the stickers at the back of the book.

57

STRANGE PICTURES

In the 1920s, a group of artists known as the Surrealists started making unusual artworks. They painted surprising combinations of objects and used games to create new, unpredictable art, inspired by dreams and their imagination.

Blobs and blots

One Surrealist game was to make pictures from random ink splatters. Here are some for you to do the same.

Exquisite corpse

The Surrealists played a game called 'exquisite corpse', where people take turns to add unexpected parts to the same picture. Try it yourself by following the instructions to the right. You need at least one other player.

The aim of exquisite corpse is to make a picture like this, where different things join together in surprising ways.

Make every section as strange as you can – but don't peek at the finished sections until the end!

How to play:

1. Cut out the opposite page where shown. (There is enough paper for two games).

2. Fill in the top section. Then, fold the paper down to the first line and pass it to the next player.

3. The next player fills in the second section, then folds the paper down to the line below.

4. Pass the paper around until each section is complete. Then, unfold it to reveal your picture.

Make sure
your drawings
continue just
below these lines.

Word pictures

Some Surrealists made pictures or shapes out of words, which they called 'calligrammes'. Try making your own below.

This sun is filled with words that describe it.

Fill the flames from this rocket with explosive sound effects.

Here are some ideas:
BOOM
KABLAM
BANG
ZOOM

You could fill the cloud with a sentence or a line from a poem about clouds, such as: "I wandered lonely as a cloud..."

Fill this crescent with words to do with the moon.

Draw with your eyes shut

The Surrealists tried to make random pictures by not thinking about, or even looking at, what they were drawing. You could try this below. Start with the tip of your pencil on the dot, then close your eyes and doodle something without taking it off the page.

You could add extra bits to whatever you doodle, to make it into something else, like this bird.

Strange combinations

The Surrealists also made collages by cutting up pictures and combining them in unusual ways. This was meant to make you look at things with fresh eyes and think about them differently. One Surrealist said art should be:

> "As beautiful as the chance meeting on a dissecting-table of a sewing-machine and an umbrella."

You can make your own Surrealist collage below using the pictures on the opposite page.

POP ART

In the 1960s, some artists began to make pictures inspired by everyday objects and 'popular' images such as advertisements, comics and even food. This became known as Pop art.

Soup-doku

Pop artist Andy Warhol created a series of pictures of Campbell's soup cans. Can you find a way to fill in the blank cans so that each line, row and box has one can of each colour?

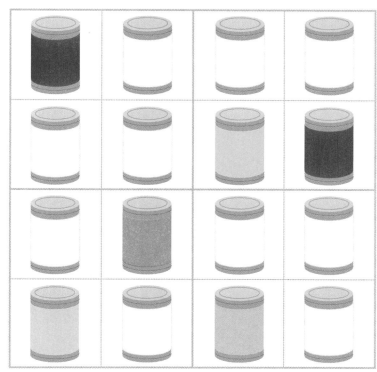

Did you know?

Warhol said he ate Campbell's soup every day for lunch for 20 years.

Screen print sneakers

Warhol used a method called screen printing to repeat the same image lots of times in different colours. Colour in these sneakers to create your own Pop art picture.

STICK PEOPLE

This picture shows crowds of thin, stick-like people on their way to watch a football match in a city. Notice how the people all look much the same. The artist may have painted them this way to suggest how life in cities can feel unfriendly or anonymous.

Going to the Match (1946)
by L. S. Lowry

Can you spot four little black dogs, one red flag, and one man walking *away* from the match?

Drawing stick people

A stick person is made up of...

an oval head...

a triangular body...

...and thick lines for arms and legs.

You could try drawing your own stick people on the opposite page.

You could draw them in different outfits...

...or doing different actions, such as kicking a ball...

...running...

...walking away...

...or hurrying along.

This dog has a sausage-shaped body, an oval head and four short legs.

Stick people city

Fill this city with stick people. You could also add lamp posts, doodle smoke coming from the chimneys, or colour in the buildings.

Did you know?

Landscapes that show city buildings and streets instead of scenes from nature are often known as 'cityscapes'.

COMIC BOOK ART

Comic books tell stories using images, speech bubbles and sound effects. Some Pop artists, such as Roy Lichtenstein, took images from comic books and enlarged them to create huge, dramatic paintings.

Going dotty

Old 1950s and 60s comic books used lots of coloured dots, called Ben-Day dots, to create different shades.

Use a felt pen to fill in the dots on this picture of a face.

You could use these dotty effects:

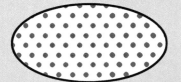

Widely spaced red dots create an impression of pink.

Blue and red dots create an impression of purple.

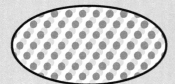

Blue and yellow dots create an impression of green.

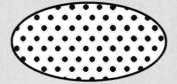

Widely spaced black dots create an impression of grey.

Did you know?

Lichtenstein added big Ben-Day dots to his pictures by painting through a stencil with lots of holes.

KAPOW!

Comic books use sound effects to add drama. Which of these would you put in each frame?

○ **CRACK!**

○ Tatatatat

○ Varooom...

○ DRING DRING

THE PHONE! WHO COULD IT BE?

TYPE THE SECRET PASSWORD, QUICK!

HE RACED ACROSS THE FROZEN LAKE BUT THE ICE WAS TOO THIN...

Spies and secrets

Here are two scenes or 'frames' from a comic book. Fill in the speech bubbles, then draw something you think might be in the briefcase.

Sizing up

Artists sometimes use grids
to enlarge or 'size up' images.
Try copying this picture of a
robot, square by square, into
the bigger grid below.

It is usually easier to enlarge
a picture one square at a time,
rather than copying it all at once.

Unfinished fram

Finish off the frames or
next page using bright
colours or Ben-Day dots
could add an alien inva
in a spacecraft, a futuri
city or a zooming super.
There's a sound effect c
the sticker pages for you
colour, too.

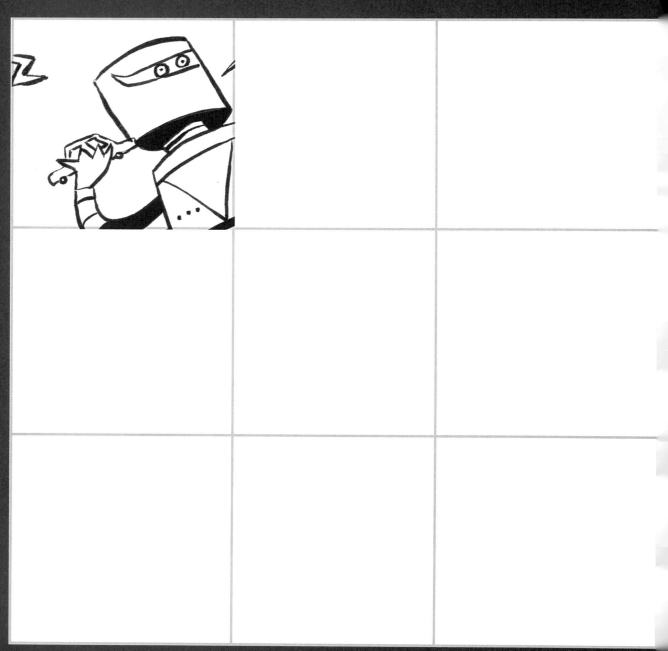

LOTS OF DOTS

Japanese artist Yayoi Kusama is well known for making large sculptures of everyday things, such as pumpkins and flowers, and then completely covering them in dots.

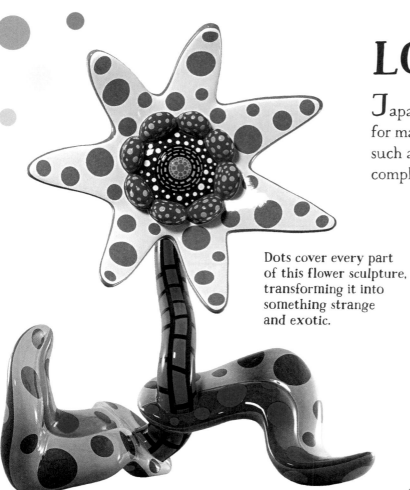

Dots cover every part of this flower sculpture, transforming it into something strange and exotic.

Flowers that Bloom Tomorrow (2010)
by Yayoi Kusama

Simple patterns

Fill in this sculpture with your own dots (or squares or stars, or other shapes).

It feels as if this flower is watching me...

Kusama sudoku

The same objects appear again and again in Kusama's work. Some of the most common are shown below. Can you fill in the grid so that each row, column and box of four squares contains one of each object?

Eye

Pumpkin

Shoe

Flower

Did you know?

Kusama once fitted a room with mirrors, then filled it with coloured lights – so the reflections looked as though they went on forever.

I'll call it the 'Infinity Room'.

Dot invasion

Sometimes, Kusama covers whole rooms and furniture in dots. You can do the same with the furniture below, using dots from the sticker pages.

Infinity maze

Oh no! A girl is lost in the Infinity Room. Can y help her find the exit? She needs to pass the ligh in this order: red, yellow, blue, orange, purple a green, without going backwards.

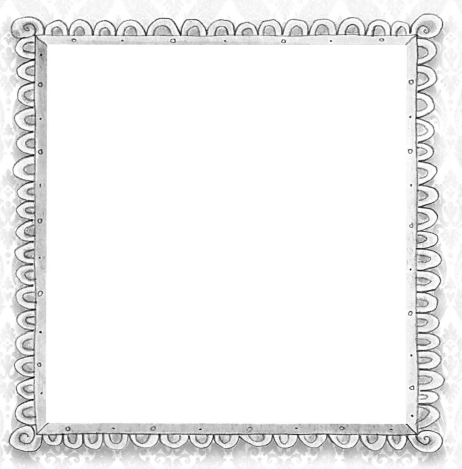

FILL THE FRAMES

Fill the empty frames in this gallery with anything from portraits to patterns.

ANSWERS & SOLUTIONS

4-5 ARTIST'S STUDIO

Starting off:

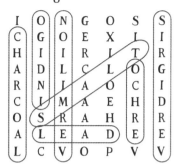

Top models:
Giovanni has copied the pose most accurately.

6-7 PORTRAITS

A = Self Portrait
B = A Man with a Wreath
C = Johann Friedrich the Magnanimous
D = Johann the Steadfast
E = Portrait of Elena Carafa

Dressed to impress:

ALPTTEE = palette
SHRBUES = brushes
SWATR ATH = straw hat
WHSLA = shawl
SLOWFER = flowers
SGNIRERA = earrings

Artistic licence:

10-11 STILL LIFES

Odd one out:

This detail is the odd one out:

Match the meaning:

1 = roses
2 = skull
3 = butterflies and bees
4 = books
5 = lilies
6 = sword
7 = candle
8 = clock

12-13 COLOURS

Paint hunt:

22-23 PERSPECTIVE

Up close:

◯ = carpet on a wall
◯ = hanging bird cage
◯ = model of a town
◯ = woman in blue
◯ = child in a white cap
◯ = apple and gourd
◯ = dovecote

Impossible perspective:

Horizon line slopes at an impossible angle

Giant lady in background gives flower to man in foreground

Laundry goes behind car

Oddly sloping window ledge

Tiles and cars are larger the further away they are

24-25 GODS AND MONSTERS

Things to spot:

- ⭕ = chariot pulled by cheetahs
- ⭕ = ring of stars
- ⭕ = Bacchus
- ⭕ = Ariadne
- ⭕ = boat sailing away in the distance

Guess the goddess:

Athena

Artemis

Aphrodite

26-27 KNIGHTS AND DRAGONS

Out of order:

The path to victory:

28-29 AT THE RACES

The race begins:

Molly Longlegs wins the race.

Horse anatomy:

There are 8 body parts in the rosette: mane, hoof, tail, back, knee, shoulder, flank, nose.

30-31 ON THE ICE

Lots to spot:

- ⭕ = man putting on skates
- ⭕ = people slipping on the ice
- ⭕ = horse and sleigh
- ⭕ = couples skating hand in hand
- ⭕ = child in a white cap

Snowmen:

Sweets and treats: gingerbread, spiced apples, plum cakes, hot pies, fruit and nuts

32-33 FABULOUS FASHION

Luxurious accessories:
- ⭕ = fans ⭕ = gold necklace
- ⭕ = ring ⭕ = brooch
- ⭕ = gold bracelets with red gemstones

Timeless fashion:

1 = C, 2 = B, 3 = A

Mirror, mirror:

B is the correct reflection.

Out of place:

The five things that don't belong are: a lamp, headphones, a smart phone, a digital watch, and a modern magazine.

34-35 ON THE RIVER

Bare boats:
The blue sail would be the most eye-catching. The red oar would look the brightest.

Sail search:

Shadow ships:

38-39 SUMMERTIME

In profile:
B is the matching profile.

On the river bank:
The man's clothes are in pile B.

Spotting challenge:

- ⬤ There are 5 boats on the river.
- ◯ Here is the little brown dog.
- ◯ There is 1 orange hat.

You can spot the factory billowing smoke at the back of the scene.

40-41 DREAM WORLDS

Theatrical flowers:
NPAYS = pansy, ISAYD = daisy, ORMSERAY = rosemary, LIVEOT = violet, LENNFE = fennel

42-43 IN THE JUNGLE

Spot the plants:

Jungle jumble:
CROCOPOTAMUS = crocodile + hippopotamus
ORANGUNKEY = orangutan + monkey
PARROPARD = parrot + leopard
ELEPHOCEROS = elephant + rhinoceros
PYTHORILLA = python + gorilla

44-47 DECORATIVE ART

Lavish accessories:

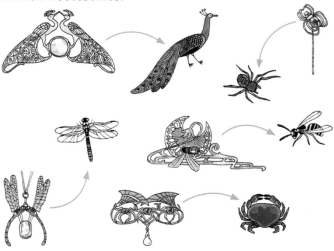

Bold shapes:
These objects are in the Art Deco style:

48-51 CUBISM

Things to spot:

- ◯ = bottle
- ◯ = glass
- ◯ = pipe
- ◯ = table
- ◯ = newspaper

Wonky portraits:
A and C were used to make the portrait.

Cubist city:

Home

Art gallery

53 ANIMAL JUMBLES

Lots of foxes:
There are 7 jumbled-up foxes.

54-55 BUILDING BLOCKS

Spot the blocks:

- ◯ = A
- ◯ = B
- ◯ = C
- ◯ = D
- ◯ = E
- ◯ = F

65 POP ART

Soup-doku:

66-67 STICK PEOPLE

- = little black dogs
- ◯ = red flag
- ◯ = man walking away from the match

68-71 COMIC BOOK ART

KAPOW!
CRACK! = D   Varooom... = A
Tatatatat = C   Dring dring = B

72-73 LOTS OF DOTS

Kusama sudoku:

Infinity maze:

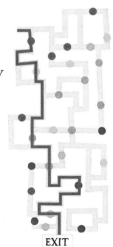

EXIT

ACKNOWLEDGEMENTS

Every effort has been made to trace the copyright holders of the material in this book. If any rights have been omitted, the publishers offer their sincere apologies and will rectify this in any subsequent editions following notification. The publishers are grateful to the following organisations and individuals for their contributions and permission to reproduce material:

Cover: *Bathers at Asnières* by Seurat, see credit for pages 38-39. Pages 6-7: *Self Portrait in a Straw Hat* by Vigée Le Brun © The National Gallery, London. *A Man with a Wreath* by Greco-Roman artist © The National Gallery, London. *Portrait of Elena Carafa* by Degas © The National Gallery, London. *Portrait of Johann Friedrich the Magnanimous* by Cranach the Elder © The National Gallery, London. *Portrait of Johann the Steadfast* by Cranach the Elder © The National Gallery, London. Pages 10-11: *Flowers in a Vase* by van Brussel © The National Gallery, London. Detail from *A Still Life of Flowers in a Wan-Li Vase* by Bosschaert the Elder © The National Gallery, London. Pages 12-13: *Sunflowers* by Van Gogh © The National Gallery, London. *Combing the Hair* by Degas © The National Gallery, London. Pages 14-15: *Orange (Roethel 180)* by Kandinsky, 1923 (lithograph printed in colours), Private Collection/Photo © Christie's Images/Bridgeman Images. Pages 16-17: *The Wilton Diptych* by an unknown artist © The National Gallery, London. Pages 18-19: *A Wheatfield, with Cypresses* by Van Gogh © The National Gallery, London. *The Cornfield* by Constable © The National Gallery, London. *La Ferté* by Bonington © The National Gallery, London. *Water-Lily Pond* by Monet © The National Gallery, London. Pages 22-23: *The Avenue at Middelharnis* by Hobbema © The National Gallery, London. *The Annunciation, with Saint Emidius* by Crivelli © The National Gallery, London. Pages 24-25: *Bacchus and Ariadne* by Titian © The National Gallery, London. Pages 26-27: *Saint George and the Dragon* by Uccello © The National Gallery, London. Pages 28-29: *Whistlejacket* by Stubbs © The National Gallery, London. Pages 30-31: *A Winter Scene with Skaters near a Castle* by Avercamp © The National Gallery, London. Pages 32-33: *Madame Moitessier* by Ingres © The National Gallery, London. Pages 34-35: *The Skiff* by Renoir © The National Gallery, London. Pages 38-39: *Bathers at Asnières* by Seurat © The National Gallery, London. Pages 40-41: *Ophelia among the Flowers* by Redon © The National Gallery, London. Pages 42-43: *Surprised!* by Rousseau © The National Gallery, London. Pages 48-49: *The Bottle of Banyuls* by Gris, 1914 (gouache & collage), Kunstmuseum, Bern, Switzerland/Peter Willi/Bridgeman Images. Pages 52-53: *The Fox* by Marc, 1913, Museum Kunstpalast Düsseldorf, Germany/Bridgeman Images. Pages 54-55: *Castle and Sun* by Klee, 1928 (no 201) (oil on canvas), Private Collection/Bridgeman Images. Pages 66-67: *Going to the Match* by Lowry, Christie's Images Limited. oil on panel, 28 x 49.5cm © 2015 Christie's Images, London/Scala, Florence © The Estate of L.S. Lowry. All Rights Reserved, DACS 2015. Pages 72-73: *Flowers that Bloom Tomorrow M, 2011* by Yayoi Kusama, fiberglass reinforced plastic, metal, urethane paint, 285 x 235 x 108 cm, 112 1/4 x 92 1/2 x 42 1/2 in, Courtesy of KUSAMA Enterprise, Ota Fine Arts, Tokyo/Singapore and Victoria Miro, London © Yayoi Kusama. Photography: Stephen White. Pages 76-77: Detail from *A Still Life of Flowers in a Wan-Li Vase* by Bosschaert the Elder, see credit for pages 10-11. *The Wilton Diptych* by an unknown artist, see credit for pages 16-17. *The Annunciation, with Saint Emidius* by Crivelli, see credit for pages 22-23. *Bacchus and Ariadne* by Titian, see credit for pages 24-25. *A Winter Scene with Skaters near a Castle* by Avercamp, see credit for pages 30-31. Pages 78-79: *Madame Moitessier* by Ingres, see credit for pages 32-33. *Bathers at Asnières* by Seurat, see credit for pages 38-39. *Surprised!* by Rousseau, see credit for pages 42-43. *The Bottle of Banyuls* by Gris, see credit for pages 48-49. *Castle and Sun* by Klee, see credit for pages 54-55. Sticker Pages: *Bacchus and Ariadne* by Titian, see credit for pages 24-25. *The Skiff* by Renoir, see credit for pages 34-35. *Surprised!* by Rousseau, see credit for pages 42-43. *Ophelia among the Flowers* by Redon, see credit for pages 40-41. *Combing the Hair* by Degas, see credit for pages 12-13. *A Wheatfield, with Cypresses* by Van Gogh, see credit for pages 18-19. *Self Portrait in a Straw Hat* by Vigée Le Brun, see credit for pages 6-7. *Water-Lily Pond* by Monet, see credit for pages 18-19. *La Ferté* by Bonington, see credit for pages 18-19.

Digital manipulation by John Russell

This edition first published in 2015 by Usborne Publishing Ltd.,
Usborne House, 83-85 Saffron Hill, London EC1N 8RT, England.
www.usborne.com Copyright © 2015 Usborne Publishing Ltd. UKE.

All rights reserved. No part of this publication may be reproduced, stored in a retrieval system or transmitted in any form or by any means, electronic, mechanical, photocopying, recording or otherwise, without the prior permission of the publisher. The name Usborne and the devices ♀ 🎈 are Trade Marks of Usborne Publishing Ltd.

Build a city on page 55, using these sticker shapes.

You could use these shapes to make a Kandinsky-style picture like the one on page 14.

Arrange these paintings in
the gallery on pages 36-37.

Add these stickers to
the Cubist portrait
on page 49.

You could use
this sound effect
on page 71.

Here are lots of
dots for page 73.